The Green Revolution

Norman Nadeau

Hatherleigh Press is committed to preserving and protecting the natural resources of the Earth. Environmentally responsible and sustainable practices are embraced within the company's mission statement.

Hatherleigh Press is a member of the Publishers Earth Alliance, committed to preserving and protecting the natural resources of the planet while developing a sustainable business model for the book publishing industry.

Library of Congress Cataloging-in-Publication Data is available upon request.
ISBN: 978-1-57826-403-2

All Hatherleigh Press titles are available for bulk purchase, special promotions, and premiums. For information about reselling and special purchase opportunities, please call 1-800-528-2550 and ask for the Special Sales Manager.

Edited by Wayne A. English
Cover Design by Melanie Garmon
Layout by Charles Fowler
Photography by Paul Nash Photography

10 9 8 7 6 5 4 3 2 1

Printed in the United States

Dedication

I dedicate this book to my dear wife and lifelong friend, Cara, and to my son, Alex, for supporting me through the long hours I put into the study and applications of sustainability and environmental science.
To my father and mother who raised me on engines, transistors, capacitors, motors, and electronics.

Contents

Vision Statement

This is part of the vision statement that I presented at the Leadership In Life Institute (LILI).

- To interact with humanity by providing services and products to consumers in need, and to provide expert advice and consultation on today's current energy resources.

- To show all of humanity how viable and obtainable elements around us are for renewable energy resource management and how to better manage our global energy resources.

- To show how to use elements around us more meaningfully, and be less dependent on fossil fuel resources which contribute to global climate change and warming of our planet, thus changing the environment around us.

- To help develop anti-intermittent renewable energy processes.

- To help, mentor, and educate people and businesses by showing them how to implement renewable energy devices and controls.

- To form a company, or co-operative, that educates, conducts energy audits and site surveys, and implements, installs, and monitors renewable energy systems. This company will be formed by government and small business initiatives using funds from private sources, grants, and for-profit, and non-profit entities.

- Lastly, to provide on-site and mobile demonstration models for public education of renewable energy technologies and how they may be implemented.

Illustration by C. Fowler

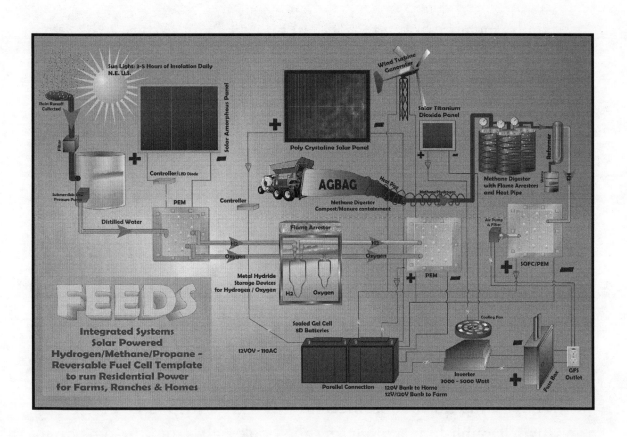

Sun Light: 3-5 Hours of Insolation Daily N.E. U.S.

Wind Turbine Generator

Rain Runoff Collected

Solar Titanium Dioxide Panel

Filter

Solar Amorphous Panel

Poly Crystaline Solar Panel

Reformer

Methane Digester with Flame Arrestors and Heat Pipe

Submersible Pressure Pump

Controller/LED Diode

PEM

Controller

Heat Pipe

AGBAG

Methane Digestor Compost/Manure containment

Methane/Hydrogen

Air Pump & Filter

Distilled Water

Flame Arrestor

H2

H2

Oxygen

Oxygen

SOFC/PEM

Metal Hydride Storage Devices for Hydrogen / Oxygen

H2

Oxygen

PEM

Sealed Gel Cell 6D Batteries

Cooling Fan

FEEDS

Integrated Systems Solar Powered Hydrogen/Methane/Propane - Reversable Fuel Cell Template to run Residential Power for Farms, Ranches & Homes

12VOV - 110AC

Parallel Connection

120V Bank to Home 12V/120V Bank to Farm

Inverter 3000 - 5000 Watt

Fuse Box

GFS Outlet

Acknowledgments

This book took three months to write, pre-edit, edit, and put all the photographs together. It had taken 13 years of studies and smart labor to compile all this data and completion of projects. We would like to thank the following people for their dedication and contributions, without which this book could not have been created.

My family members—Cara, Alex, Omi, Jack, and Arbus, who were patient with me, once again, sharing with me the time-consuming process of creating a book. Thanks again for giving the space, time, and emotional support needed to follow my passion. I would like to thank Charles Fowler for the endless hours of graphics work reconstructing my hand-written schematics of integration and inventions.

Wayne English, who edited my manuscript and coached me through the first edition. Wayne put in lots of time, effort, and good advice. To Paul Nash Photography, who made a leap of faith to shoot still photography for my project which came out great.

Kathleen Keegan, who is my public relations manager and has coached me through to the next stage of public speaking and helped me market these books and make future appearances. Melanie Garmon, who created the cover art, oh so patiently, and gave me wonderful advice to guide me in publishing this book. Melanie was a great help. She directed me towards self-publishing and getting the book right from the outside in. Bob Gould, who helped out with the hydrogen hybrid cars, which we had lots of fun with. Pace.org has been a part of this project, and I want to give thanks to Judi Freedman. 350.org has also been a supporter of "Project FEEDS".

Foreword

Earth, the Beginning Frontier

Now we must live with what we have and preserve the future of humankind, to sustain our energy future and the resources around us. Mankind has commercialized our use of resources for 2,000 years. For the last 100 years we have used petroleum resources which pollute the Earth and may permanently damage it unless we, as sophisticated animal organisms, reverse the pollution in our air (or rising carbon monoxide, also known as CO_2). Things are heating up here on planet Earth. Humans call it global warming. We must be symbiotic with planet Earth and its rich resources, especially renewable and natural resources.

Preface

The book of Genesis says that in the beginning God created the heavens and the Earth. Then the Lord God planted the Garden of Eden, and placed Man in the Garden to cultivate and care for it. God looked at everything he had made, and found it very good.

Let this be the guidance for humans to preserve all resources we are given here and to sustain our quality of life with abundance. Unfortunately, our human race has long polluted our environment. We have been given the privilege to have and hold everything around us, but we have become wasteful and greedy. Now we want to clean it up. Humans have made the wrong energy choices over a span of 150 years or more. There has been more pollution, waste, and human accidents which have inadvertently harmed the Earth and wronged our own race. These choices have almost annihilated our chance for giving our future generations energy sustainability and food. Don't forget peace, water, and anything else needed for humans to begin finding the next Earth and/or the next frontier. We hope that humans can exist for another 1,000 years or more, but this can happen only if we are wise in making energy choices that are renewable and selecting food sources that can be reproduced and sustained. Scientists say the Earth is only able to hold around four billion people, yet now there are seven billion. One billion humans will be affected by global warming in the future, and many will die, unfortunately, during migrations while trying to seek a new way of life.

There are three kinds of humans on this planet Earth: those who wait, those who watch, and those who do. Which one are you? It's okay to be the first to test the waters and to take the sometimes inherent risks. Being a pioneer, or a good-for-humankind revolutionary, is being the kind of person who is willing to try to sustain himself and others around him. Welcome to "The Green Revolution", the new way of human living, the way of setting precedence to forge our way to the heavens and to all realms of our universe. It all starts with Earth, then our moon, then Mars, then the outer reaches, then other galaxies and beyond, but only if we learn how to conserve the ecosystems that we cohabit with. In this book are many ways to adapt to a new way of living carbon-negative.

—Norman A. Nadeau

Visionary/Philosopher

The Technology

Solar-Powered Watch

This is my solar-powered Citizen™ Eco-Drive, wristwatch. It will hold a charge for up to six months. This watch lasts up to 50 years without batteries, winding, or kinetic movement. This watch can replace all the many watches you have gone through in a lifetime, watches that will inevitably end up in a landfill. Let us all learn from this futuristic timepiece, which is available today.

Light-Emitting Diode

A light-emitting diode (LED) is an electronic part that only lets electrical currentgoinonedirectiontopreventelectricalcurrentfromgoingbackwards. If the current went backwards it would short out electronic components. A light-emitting diode will protect electrical circuits, lasts 10,000 hours or more, and takes substantially less energy to power, resulting in less energy waste than conventional electric bulbs. They come in many different sizes and colors and can be powered at any voltage and/or wattage. My family has them on our ranch and in our lives, lighting everywhere we go. Get ready to adapt to a new way of lighting our future.

Rechargeable Batteries

Rechargeable batteries can be recharged many times before they need replacement. They are the same size as alkaline batteries and can replace alkaline and other conventional batteries that pollute our landfills and the environment. Traditional batteries must be thrown away after just one use. What a waste! They also contain lead and toxic alkaline materials that emit harmful chemicals.

Rechargeable batteries are becoming more evolved and powerful as technology advances. There will be alternative and more advanced energy storage devices that will even replace the rechargeable batteries that we have today. These newer batteries are made from nickel-metal hydride, NiMH. Also, lithium batteries possess great rechargeable qualities. There will be a next generation battery that will even supersede this generation of storage batteries. Out with the old, in with the new. Here are your usual old style batteries that we used to throw away after just one use. What a waste! They are thrown away and make their way to the dump. They contain lead and toxic alkaline materials that emit harmful chemicals. These batteries are dead and are only good for this picture. The new portable power source is rechargeable, and the next generation of battery is on its way. Most battery manufacturers that make alkaline batteries also make the new rechargeable batteries.

Photo-Voltaic Solar Array

Here is the beginning of installing solar electric grid-tie systems on homes. Each of us, homeowners and business owners alike, will become micro-electricity producers, supplying renewable power for today's and tomorrow's energy needs.

This solar array is an 8kw (8,000 watt) grid-tied hybrid amorphous solar array. These photo-voltaic cells work well in low light conditions, cloudy days, and of course, on sunny days. You can exchange your current corporate energy bill with a renewable energy bill that shouldn't increase in yearly costs, cost of living increases, or increased crude oil prices. You can qualify for tax credits of up to 30%, produce green power, emit no CO_2 emissions, and be self-sustainable. It feels good to have a $20.25 monthly electric bill. That's the price for having the right to produce, store, and sell kilowatts over the electric grid. Now we have fixed the price of energy in the form of kilowatt credits for the next 15 years for our homestead. You can too! Welcome to the Green Revolution.

Triple-Base Solar Array (top)
Basement Grid-Tie Inverter and Production Meter (bottom)

23

Off-Grid Inverter vs. Grid-Tied Inverter

Here are inverters that convert DC (direct current) to AC (alternating current). All electronic devices that use a cord need AC current. The top inverter, pictured here, converts solar DC current to AC current and then sends it to the home. Any excess energy that is generated goes into the power lines or grid through a metered device that tracks the taken kilowatts to be purchased back at a later time.

The other inverter converts DC to AC current to run the farm. This is an off-grid inverting system for producing and storing electricity. The renewable energy created is inverted into watts and is stored in large batteries-in-series, to be used at a later time.

Grid-Tied Inverter (top)
Off-Grid Inverter (bottom)

Hydrogen Fuel Cell Experiment Car

Here is a kit that you can put together to learn the basics of hydrogen fuel cells. You can modify the kit to run many things such as fans, motors, and LEDs.

"What the mind of man can conceive and believe, it can achieve."

— Napoleon Hill

Wind Turbine

The Earth spins on an axis. This rotation creates the jet streams around our globe and thus creates wind. Heat that emanates from the continents and oceans also creates wind. Every season produces wind, some places all the time and some places very infrequently. Man must harness this renewable resource regardless of how infrequent or irregular and integrate wind power along with all other potential renewable energies. This will solve the problem of intermittent generation surrounding many renewable energy systems.

Here is a 24v, 1kw (1,000 watt) micro-wind turbine which is part of a hybrid renewable energy system. It operates when storms come through, and more often in the fall and winter months. On windy days we harness the energy of the wind. This type of system is for remote areas.

Also needed with the wind turbine is an inverter and electronics. There are 215 watt hybrid amorphous solar panels accompanying the turbine. There is a 2,000 watt inverter with remote control and four batteries, connected in series, with a charger controller to maintain the battery backup.

Wind Turbine (top)
Hybrid Energy Box (bottom)

29

Solar Hot Water—Indirect Solar Thermal Heating

Solar hot water is another way to use the sun to heat water for human use and consumption. Most systems like this one can take care of up to 80% of the energy used to heat the water in your home, thus lowering the cost and dependency on fossil fuels and nuclear power. These systems are a first alternative toward going green because of lower fuel costs. When done properly, there is a 30% tax credit on all solar thermal systems of mostly any kind here in the United States. Geothermal hot water and cooling systems can also qualify for government tax credits.

This solar hot water system uses evacuated tubes and does not rely solely on direct sunlight. Only radiant light is needed to generate the necessary heat. This solar hot water system is computer programmable and can be easily adjusted to suit the individual household or business. The fluid used to deliver heat to the stone tank is propylene glycol, a vegetable-based fluid that is nontoxic to the environment. There is a variable flow pump which only turns on when there is a temperature difference between the rooftop mounted evacuated tubes and the stone-lined hot water storage tank located in the basement. It is extremely efficient and quite ingenious. I did it, you can do it too.

Solar Evacuated Tubes (top)
Storage Tanks and Controls (bottom)

31

Ecofan™: It Works Without Wires!

Here is a way to increase the efficiency of a wood furnace or stove. An Ecofan™ has a thermo-couple, so the fan gets its energy from heat through a bi-electric metal plate that transfers heat, which agitates ion molecules. This, in turn, produces electricity and powers the fan through heat radiating from a heat source like a wood stove or hot pipes. This model comes from Canada and can be readily purchased online. Thank you, Canada, for letting us purchase and use this wireless and efficient device to circulate heat around the house. This sort of device works like a sterling engine, based on the heat transfer method to change energy into motion. Efficiency is increased by almost 40% for furnaces or stoves. When the fan slows down it is a sign that more fuel is needed. This is a must for any wood stove.

Hallway of Light

The lights in our hallway are illuminated by LEDs (light-emitting diodes). This is soft lighting that is low wattage. These lights will last more than 10,000 hours and are very reliable. These lights get a great deal of use in a home.

Using Methane

Here is a methane extraction template using a manure compost pile. The anaerobic bacterium decomposes manure, thus creating heat and methane gas. The methane gas is extracted from the compost pile in several ways. One method is to reform the methane into hydrogen for fuel cell use. The hydrogen can then be stored for usage at a later time. Methane can also be used for cooking when burned in a propane generator or grill. Landfills in Connecticut use similar systems to trap and reuse methane gases to generate electricity.

If released into the atmosphere, methane gas can create 20 times more carbon dioxide than most bio-fuels. That's why capturing, reforming, and/or burning it for energy usage is very important. Methane can be organically created via manure, captured, and carefully stored for future uses. Working with methane gas can be explosive and hazardous, so take precautions and think "safety first".

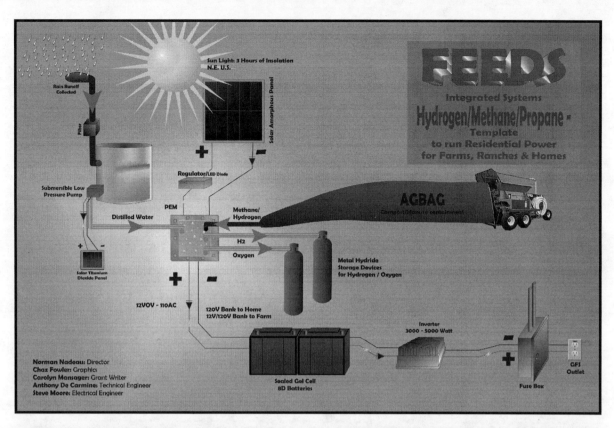

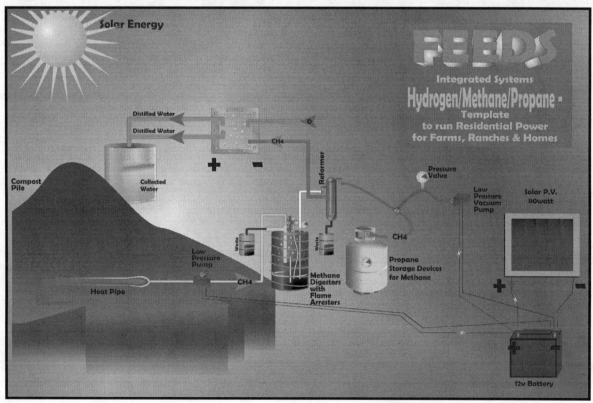

Methane Extraction for Fuel Cell Use (top)
Methane Extraction and Reformation (bottom)

37

Homopolar Motor

Here is a homopolar motor, perhaps the simplest motor you can build. My son and I came across one of these on a video at YouTube.com. We decided to build one with one magnetic pole, a battery, and a copper wire. The magnet that we used is not a typical magnet. It is a neodymium magnet, a rare Earth magnet, and very powerful. The batteries are rechargeable and I used a heavy gauge copper wire shaped like a heart. Have fun trying to balance the moving rotating wire. You can have a blast building one with your children while showing them the principles of magnetism and energy. Just remember to remove the wire from the assembly when not in use, as the wire gets hot if left unattended and could melt the battery.

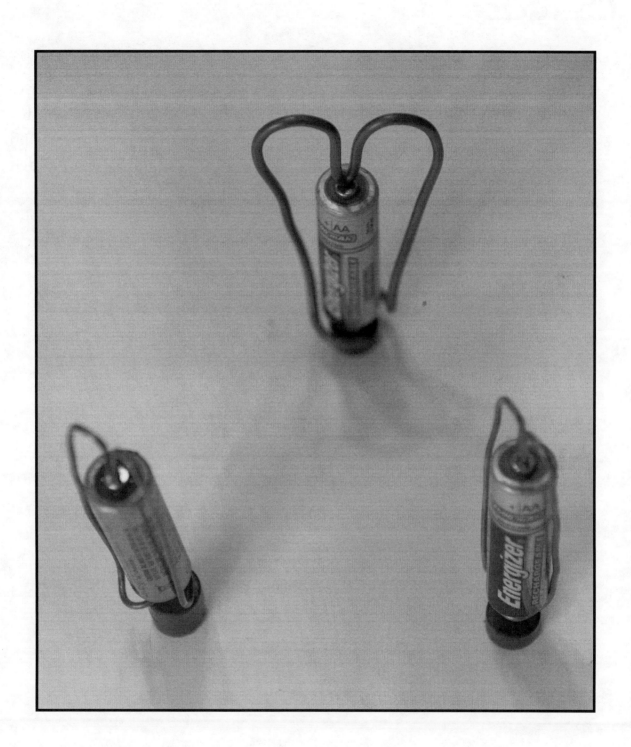

Rechargeable Batteries and Solar Battery Chargers

Solar battery chargers are a good way to use rechargeable batteries and receive free energy from the sun. Batteries are a necessity for all of our modern gadgets. Using rechargeable batteries is a must, and the capability to use solar battery chargers for recharging is an added bonus. Remember, rechargeable batteries will recharge over 1,000 times versus old alkaline batteries that are used once and then thrown out. This is a practical way to utilize renewable resources wisely, with less waste.

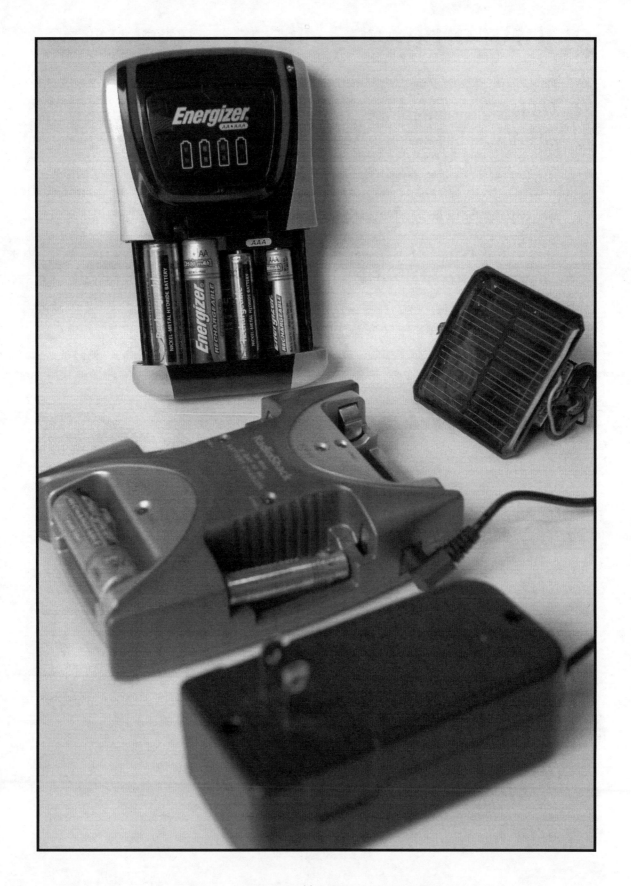

Solar Amorphous Silicon Panel

Here is a solar amorphous silicon panel. This dark-bodied panel works well in low light conditions and in direct sunlight. Amorphous panels take in lots of light, or photons, to move ions in the photo-sensitive material, creating an electrical current. Hybrid panels are now available that utilize amorphous panels for low light conditions.

I use these types of panels all around the farm. They work well for recharging batteries of all sizes. They make good mirrors, as you can see here.

43

Monocrystalline Solar Panel

Here is a monocrystalline solar panel; these were the first solar panels made to generate electricity from the sun. I call them the 'old dinosaur solar panels'. They have evolved to require less usage of silicon and are manufactured more efficiently. Now there is a photo-voltaic medium called nano solar paint, as well as other kinds of nano solar products that are prevailing over these old panels.

The life expectancy of these monocrystalline panels is 25-30 years. Towns and municipalities sometimes try to dispose of these old panels, and you can find and re-use them. They will still work, but not as efficiently, and could be free if you can find them. You can also find them at discount prices online.

LED Flashlights

Most new flashlights are made with LEDs (light-emitting diodes). They are bright and have lots of lumens just like the old incandescent flashlight bulbs.

These are run by rechargeable batteries. At my farm, we only use LED flashlights, and you will start to see them all around your life. They are now being used in traffic lights and are appearing in new automobiles and homes. As they grow in popularity, pricing of these LED bulbs are being reduced. Once again, tax credits abound for updating your lighting.

Solar-Powered LED Lights

Here are two pets you will never have to feed; they provide you with green accent lighting on your deck or doorstep. They are affordable, efficient, reliable, and look very cool. Sunlight charges them and they store energy in rechargeable batteries. They can recharge over 1,000 times. The technology of solar-powered lights is getting better. They now have fiber optic solar-powered lighting and solar panels that run by fiber optics. The solar panels of the future will no longer need to be in direct sunlight.

Rechargeable Computer with Wireless Mouse

Here is a computer that is recharged over and over. Most laptops today use lithium-ion rechargeable batteries. This picture also shows a rechargeable wireless mouse, which is powered by two AA NiMH rechargeable batteries. Computers and peripheral hardware use a lot of wattage to run them. Here I am using a wattage monitor (the device plugged into the wall outlet) that shows the usage of recharging and running the computer. A wattage monitor can test all appliances in your household to see how efficient they are.

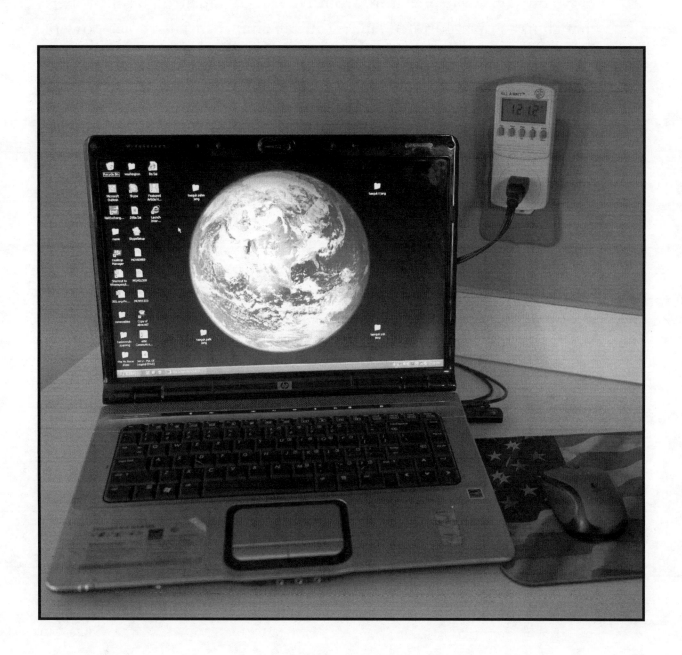

Solar-Powered Electric Fence

How do you keep predators from entering a ranch or farm property that abuts to open forested land? You can simply install a solar-powered electric fence. I installed this fence six years ago with little maintenance. I used a special electric rope and wire with switches. It is powered by the sun during the day and uses battery storage at night. Everyday this fence renews its energy and then runs all night on the battery backup. This system will not harm the inside animals if they rub or touch the electric rope or wire.

It is designed to keep out predators like coyotes, foxes, deer, bears, and cougars. All these animals have approached our fence line in the past and have not breached the inside paddocks. This proves that renewable energy sources work here in this application. No more 120v system is needed to electrify the fence and no extreme electricity bills.

Recycled Rubber Door Mat

Here we have a recycled door mat to wipe our feet. This is made of recycled tire rubber and is very tough. Processed and recycled, these are someone's used, old, and flat tires kept from burning in a dump. It works very well and is ergonomically fitting for a welcome mat.

The next time you change the tires on your car, remember to recycle your tires with responsibility, and think of obtaining this or similar recycled items for your home or business.

Ecological Dishwashing Fluid

Here is a great way to wash your dishes. It is an eco-friendly dishwashing washing liquid made from plant-based ingredients. It is completely biodegradable and was not tested on animals. You can find it at most grocery stores. Now *that's* green.

The Water Bottle

Here is the infamous water bottle. Every where you go you will see water bottles being sold, trashed, or dropped on the ground like dirty cigarette butts. These plastic containers can be reused and recycled. Most states now pay .10 cents for refund of all water and beverage containers. Now that's sustainability. Different plastics are made in different grades of polyethylene. A number 1 recycling symbol on the bottom of the bottle means that it won't emit as much toxic carcinogens and chemicals through the plastics into your water or food in comparison to other grade plastics. You might have tasted this before from a favorite drink in a plastic container.

Let this be a lesson on human consumption of beverages, and hopefully, it will make you think twice before buying your next drink held in a plastic bottle. Remember to strive for peace and tranquility, with a clean environment to go with it.

Recycled Reusable Grocery Bags

You have likely seen these at grocery stores, the newest green wave to reduce plastic and paper waste. These convenient grocery bags are made from recycled materials for grocery shopping or for general use. Reusable bags are occasionally free or offered at a low cost of around $1.00. You can find them in larger grocery stores. They prevent millions and millions of wasted, one-time-use plastic and paper bags from entering the landfills of America and abroad. Some stores have even started to charge a fee for their plastic bags that were once always free (and which end up in the landfill). To counter this, some grocery stores now offer you a small discount for each recycled bag that you use when shopping; how about that? Incentive!

So what should you do with all those plastic bags? There are also some stores which offer collection bins to properly recycle them.

EcoPens

Here are EcoPens, which are made here in America by Acme Studio, Inc. in Hawaii. These pens are pretty cool because they are biodegradable, all-natural, and made of corn starch plastic. The pens come in a variety of colors, all of which use black soy ink. These pens will breakdown and decompose in a year if they end up on the ground or make it to a landfill. This sets the precedence for the future on penmanship.

Recycled Plastic Deck

My hydrogen fuel cell car sits upon the rail of my recycled composite-material constructed deck. Everyone who needs to replace their deck now has the option of using fake textured wood, recycled wood, or plastic decking made from a collection of recycled plastics and recycled wood by-products. These decks are very durable, perhaps even more durable than wood decks that can warp or splinter. They also require little maintenance. Occasionally we powerwash the deck to keep it clean. For the past eight years, my deck has held up extraordinarily well in the New England winter months at our farm.

The decking material comes in a variety of colors and there are a variety of manufacturers that make this product nationwide. This product is a positive solution versus using the traditional, chemically-enhanced, pressure-treated wood decking. These decks will last a lot longer than other decks made of wood materials, with less maintenance.

Fruit and Potato Clock

Here is a fruit and potato clock that runs on vegetables or fruits (or or any combination thereof). It keeps time for months on end, especially when potatoes are used. This is a basic fuel cell battery using the acidic fluids from fruits and vegetables. It is very economical to buy and run. It is also educational for children to start learning about electrolyte cells, batteries, clocks, and electronics.

Neodymium Magnets

What are neodymium magnets? These are rare Earth magnets with a magnetic pull ten times stronger than most common magnets. These magnets have a north and south pole magnetism. Pictured here, they are being utilized to increase miles per gallon (MPG). They face each other with the south poles together, covering a hydrocarbon fuel line. This changes the valence from negative to positive and thus compresses the molecular structure of hydrocarbon liquid fuel. The south poles do not pull magnets together, but instead push apart when they face each other on the south side. You can buy these kits online for as low as $15 per set and they could increase your fuel efficiency by 2-4 MPG. They do work and I have installed them on both of my fuel cell hybrid vehicles. Nowadays, every little bit helps and these magnets are so easy to install, yet so effective. These kits can also be put on a home heating oil line, just before it reaches the furnace/boiler. They can also be put on water lines to soften water for drinking, bathing, cooking, and washing.

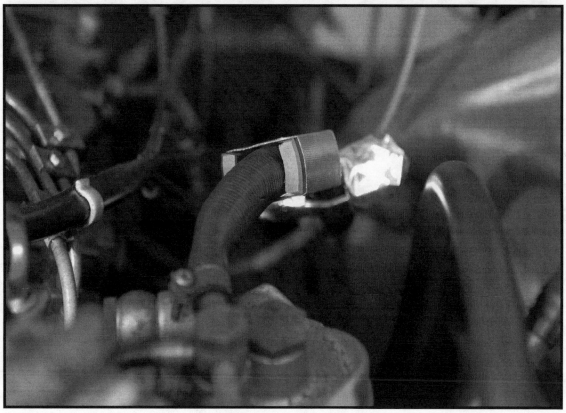

Magnets on Fuel Line of Audi A4 Quattro™ (top)
Pair of Magnets on Fuel Line of Mercedes 240D™ (bottom)

69

Reusable Automotive Air Filter

Here is a way to not to have to worry about replacing the dirty air filter on your car or truck. Today you can buy a reusable air filter that can be washed in detergent and water, then replaced after it has dried.

Initially, the reusable filter will cost twice as much as a conventional air filter that you replace each year, but after the up-front cost, you won't need to buy another air filter. In the long run, you will save money and will have less waste.

Recycled Books

Here is one of my favorite paper books called *Green, Greener, Greenest* by Lori Bongiorno. This book is an excellent guide to going, living, and staying green in our everyday lives and is also made from recycled material. Some of my greatest and most enjoyable green ideas came from this book. Please get one today at your local bookstore or an online bookstore.

"An indispensable resource for anyone trying
to reduce their environmental impact:
comprehensive and convincing but also sane and realistic."
—Michael Pollan, bestselling author of
The Omnivore's Dilemma

GREENGREENERGREENEST

A Practical Guide
to Making Eco-Smart Choices
a Part of Your Life

Lori Bongiorno

Foreword by Frances Beinecke,
President of the Natural Resources Defense Council

Green Soldering Gun

This is a new rechargeable Cold Heat™ soldering gun for small applications such as electronics. This gun works on rechargeable batteries and is an alternative to 120 VAC soldering guns. The old guns cool slowly and are a fire hazard. The Cold Heat™ soldering gun cools very fast, reducing the chance of burns, and thus is a low-risk fire hazard.

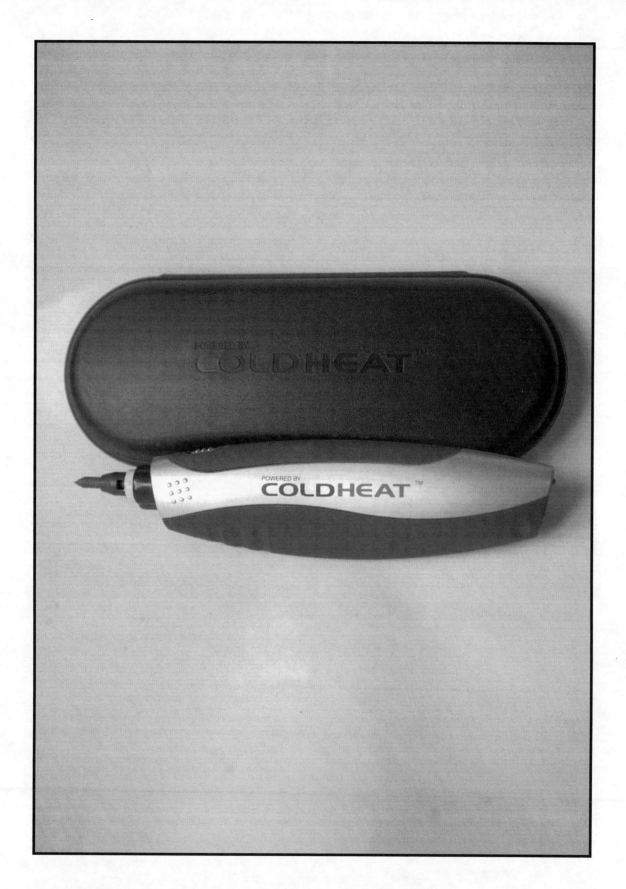

LED Timer

Here is an LED 12v timer. The electronics department at Manchester Community College made this and donated it for my hydroponic aquaculture growing system. This switch controls the circulating pump that moves water from the aquaculture to the hydroponic system. And, of course, it's run by the sun via photo-voltaic panels.

Solar Hydrogen Electrolyzer

This is a device that I made with parts from around the house. I call it a Solar Hydrogen Electrolyzer. This device produces hydrogen and oxygen during the day and can also store hydrogen and oxygen for later use. This device uses distilled water, vinegar, and a proton exchange membrane (PEM), as the fuel cell. This particular fuel cell was imported from Germany. You can buy these devices online for on-site production of hydrogen needed for a fuel cell that converts hydrogen gas back to a liquid while creating electricity. Welcome to the Green Revolution.

Caution!
Solar hydrogen Electrolyzer
No Open Flames or Sparks!
Flammable and Explosive!

Levitating Magnet Motor

Here is one of the newest inventions from ideas cultivated around the world. This is my first levitating magnet motor, which uses a combination of strong rare Earth magnets called neodymium magnets. These magnets are a challenge to work with because they are so powerful. They are ten times stronger than ordinary magnets. This device works when a series of opposing rotating rare Earth magnets challenge two discs on a spindle, causing rotation. Rotation creates the electric field that generates power to run the little electric motor. Now let's build a huge one and see what it can generate.

Farm and Ranch Lighting

Here is an economical lighting system I built from scratch for my ranch facility. These 120VAC LEDs are very low-wattage illuminators but are very bright. They use only a fraction of the energy needed for old incandescent bulbs, compact fluorescents, and halogen bulbs. They get the job done, last a long while, and are positively green.

Hydroponic Aquaculture Symbiotic Growing System

Here is a new technology that creates a symbiotic closed ecosystem, which allows you to grow fish for consumption as you would grow fresh vegetables in a garden. Hydroponics is the process of growing plants without dirt. It uses a clay medium of pebble-like balls to store nutrients that the roots grab on to. Aquaculture is the practice of farming fish and/or aquatic plants. A combination of the two is called aquaponics. My system is exactly that. It uses a solar photo-voltaic panel, battery, LED electronic timer, hydroponic float, and an oxygen cell. Every 30 minutes, this system circulates water from a fish tank to the hydroponic system that grows vegetables. The fish living in the fish tank excrete certain types of nutrients into the water, which feeds the vegetables. The plants, in turn, aerate and clean the water, which then drains back into the fish tank to supply cleaner, oxygen-enriched water. The type of fish that can be kept in this system include Koi or Tilapia. The solar-powered battery oxygen cell also helps aerate the water by infusing oxygen into the water. This system will be perfected as I build the next generation system using a Koi pond and my solar thermal greenhouse.

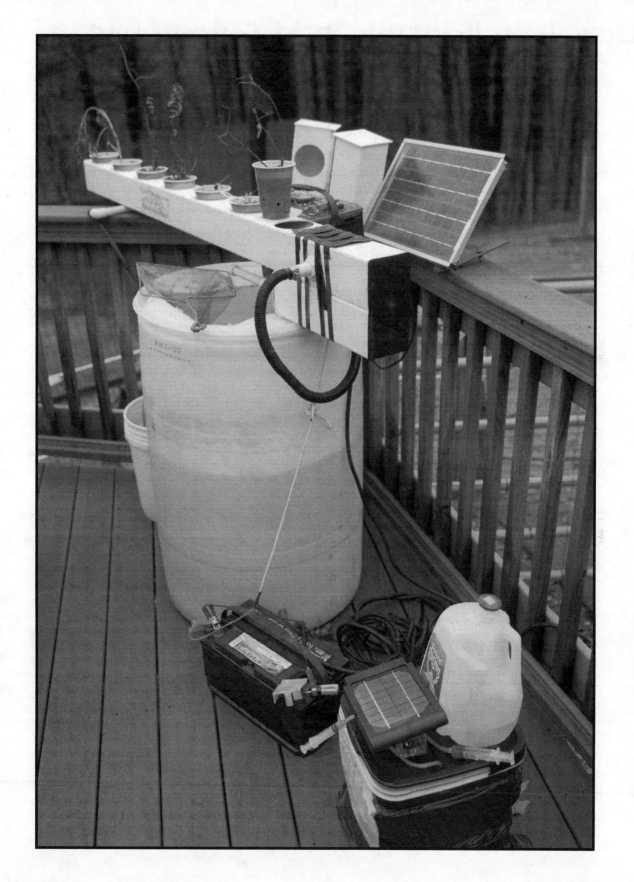

Diesel-Hydrogen Hybrid Automobile

Pictured here is a 1983 Mercedes 240D diesel automobile that has been converted into a hydrogen hybrid. This car had 34 MPG when I first bought it. We installed the Hydrogen-Hydrogen Oxygen (HHO) kit, and the car now gets around 40 MPG or more. After proper research, I found a kit online. It consists of a three-stack hydrogen fuel cell kit, which is placed in the engine compartment with a 2-liter tank of distilled water and vinegar. It took about 6 hours to install with little hassle.

I top off the distilled water tank once per week with approximately a half liter or less of solution. The results on the vehicle are:

- No more black smoke from the tailpipe
- Super low emissions
- Better fuel economy
- Cleaner interior engine, which makes a longer-lasting engine and increased horsepower.

I use vegetable-based synthetic oil in the engine instead of processed fossil fuel motor oils. This change will reduce the carbon footprint of the vehicle substantially. Please note that these kits were originally designed for large diesel tractor trailers. I wanted to try this technology to see if it could be used to improve efficiency and reduce emissions for those daily drivers using cars and trucks that jam up our highways and byways across the world. This car is featured on the testimonial page of www.cthydro.com.

Anyone can have their car converted, today, although each make and model of car or truck will be a custom installation. Get one installed today to save money and fuel, reduce engine wear, increase power, and drive a green car with an on-board hydrogen fuel cell.

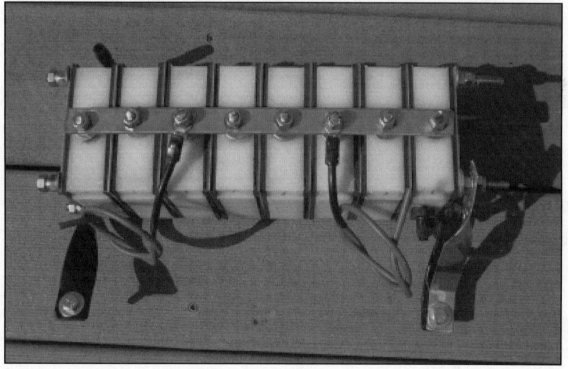

Diesel Engine Compartment of Mercedes 240D™ (top)
Fuel cell that generates Hydrogen-Hydrogen Oxygen (HHO) (bottom)

Gasoline-Hydrogen Hybrid Automobile

This is one of the first gasoline-hydrogen hybrid automobiles in Connecticut. We installed a Hydrogen-Hydrogen Oxygen (HHO) kit onto my 2004 Audi A4 Quattro 1.8 Turbo. We used a custom 8 hydrogen fuel cell stack kit for this car. We managed to install this kit to look just like the original equipment manufacture (OEM).

The results are positively staggering. The installed hydrogen fuel cell electrochemically splits distilled vinegar and distilled water inside the fuel cell to produce hydrogen. As a gas, hydrogen travels to the air plenum (also called the air intake chamber) and mixes with air and fuel. The vehicle soon has increased fuel efficiency, near zero emissions, a cleaner engine, a longer engine life, and more horsepower. This is now a green clean machine. Welcome to the Green Revolution.

Engine Compartment of the Audi A4 Quattro (top)
Rear of Vehicle (bottom)

Water and Vinegar

Here is a picture of what I use to fuel the hydrogen fuel cells in both automobiles. Have you seen these in your local grocery store? I use distilled white vinegar and distilled water, both of which can be purchased from either your local food store or at big-box stores. The water and vinegar are used as electrolytes for the fuel cells and are noncaustic (nontoxic) to the environment.

Solar Thermal Greenhouse

I built this solar thermal greenhouse from a template found at the University of Wisconsin. This is based on a model situated on the Canadian border. My version of the greenhouse measures 20' by 20' and has an 8-millimeter plastic shell around it. Fifty bales of hay make up the north wall, which is enhanced by a reflective material that directs solar rays into the greenhouse. The floor is an 18-inch bed of seasoned Alpaca manure. Due to its thermal properties, I placed approximately 600 gallons of water, stored in tanks, inside the greenhouse. These gallons of water are hooked up with a rechargeable timer for irrigation. This greenhouse grows fresh vegetables nine months out of the year, allowing us to freeze surplus vegetables for the winter months.

This greenhouse model can be made to grow vegetables year round using photo-voltaic battery chargers and batteries, fans controlled by electric sensors, and temperature switches. It can also operate automatically.

This greenhouse has enhanced our way of living, allowing my family to be independent. Welcome to the Green Revolution.

Energy Star Appliances

Ovens

Energy Star appliances are very eco-friendly. In my house they replaced the old, leaking, energy-consuming appliances that have been sold to millions, since the first revolutionary engine-powered vacuum cleaner was made available.

The government has incentives for the public to buy these new Energy Star appliances by offering tax credits and rebates. In turn, the more Energy Star appliances that are being used, the less fossil fuel that will be abused. These new, efficient products help Americans to save time and also conserve energy. Remember to recycle old units responsibly.

Energy Star Microwave (top)
Energy Star Oven Range (bottom)

Refrigerator

If not adjusted properly, a refrigerator would keep running day and night, consuming power the entire time. This is the refrigerator in my kitchen, which is an Energy Star appliance. I set the refrigeration side and freezer at level 2 so that the unit runs at an efficient moderate operating level. Because of these settings, it only needs to run about half the amount of time that it used to, and still keeps my perishables cold and frozen. Watch for these energy-saving appliances at your local stores; you can have one too. Welcome to the Green Revolution.

Dishwasher

Here is an Energy Star appliance that is new to my home. We originally had an old dishwasher that came with the house when we first purchased it. It would do its job, but it was noisy, it leaked foam, and it didn't clean effectively. This new dishwasher is three times more efficient than its counterpart (which we ultimately recycled). When we use the dishwasher, we now have clean dishes in a fast, affordable, and efficient manner. The dishwasher is quiet and reliable, and my wife really enjoys it. You want to have one of these.

Project FEEDS (Friendly Environmental Energy Dependent Systems)

Project FEEDS means Friendly Environmental Energy Dependent Systems, a hybrid of renewable energy-generating systems that are integrated to run in a synchronous manner. When one system is off, another is on to form a multitude of systems running together in full functionality. This is my original project regarding renewable energy. We use solar power, wind power, hydrogen, methane, fuel cells, battery storage, hydrogen storage, compost containment, heat pumps, solar thermal power, and of course, the electric grid as a backup. This allows us to use little or no fossil fuels for energy resources. Next, I am working on systems beyond renewable (such as cold fusion, algae blooms, infrared technology, thermoelectric generation, production synthesis gas, and super capacitors), that would make fossil fuels obsolete.

Illustration by C. Fowler

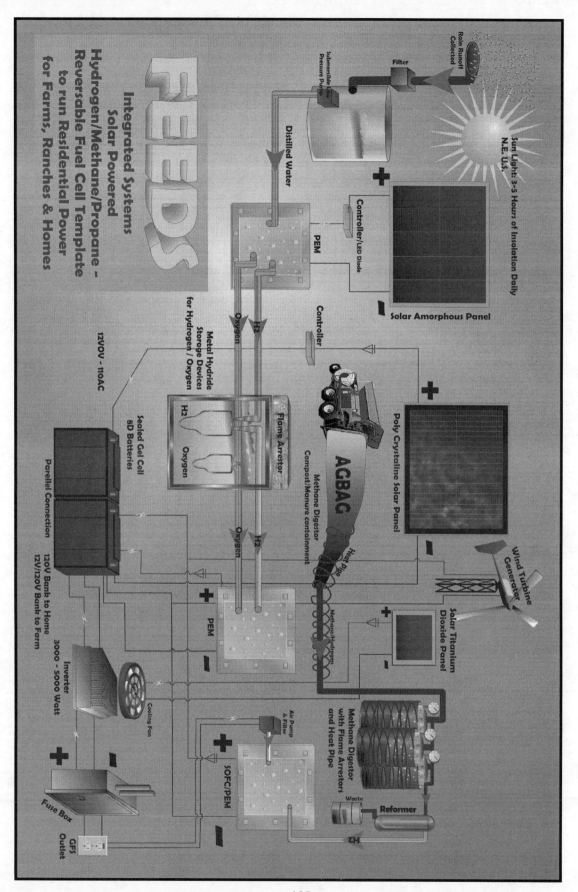

FEEDS

Integrated Systems
Solar Powered
Hydrogen/Methane/Propane –
Reversable Fuel Cell Template
to run Residential Power
for Farms, Ranches & Homes

Sun Light 3-5 Hours of Insolation Daily
N.E. U.s.

Rain Runoff
Collected

Filter

Submersible Low
Pressure Pump

Distilled Water

Controller/LED Diode

PEM

Solar Amorphous Panel

Controller

Oxygen
H2

Metal Hydride
Storage Devices
for Hydrogen / Oxygen

12V0V - 110AC

H2

Oxygen

Flame Arrestor

Sealed Gel Cell
8D Batteries

Parellel Connection

120V Bank to Home
12V/120V Bank to Farm

Inverter
3000 - 5000 Watt

Cooling Fan

Fuse Box

GFS
Outlet

Oxygen
H2

PEM

SOFC/PEM

Air Pump
& Filter

AGBAG

Methane Digestor
Compost/Manure containment

Heat Pipe

Poly Crystaline Solar Panel

Wind Turbine
Generator

Solar Titanium
Dioxide Panel

Methane/Hydrogen

Methane Digestor
with Flame Arrestors
and Heat Pipe

Reformer

Waste

H2

105

Meet the Farm Animals

Solar Fence Inhabitant

Here is one of the inhabitants of my solar electric fence community, a very exotic spider. I think this is a fiddleback or teddy bear spider. I'm sure there is a more scientific name for this particular species, and like the spider in the favorite story *Charlotte's Web*, this particular spider could make a perfect new web everyday. We had noticed that this spider would make a new web each morning along the fence line. He is quite large for local arachnids and showed up here in the fence line of the horse paddock. His web could hold droplets of water or dew in the mornings. I am sure his prey got a shocking experience.

Natural Pest Control

On our farm there is a wide range of animals that reside here. First up is one of nature's perfect hunters. Arbus, our barn cat, stays with the chickens and alpacas. He keeps rodents off our farm and ranch, which also keeps out disease-prone organisms. We get good eggs, fiber, and meat because of low disease factors thanks to our barn cat, Arbus. In this picture, Arbus is hanging out on the recycled plastic deck.

Alpacas

Jack is the guard at our farm. He is smart, inquisitive, and gentle. Jack's lineage is from Peru and he is a Huayaca alpaca. Their fleece is used to produce very warm and soft socks, gloves, hats, scarves, and blankets. In addition to providing wool, Jack also protects his herd and his human family from predators. Our animals give us unconditional love and friendship all the time. The bottom image on the facing page shows alpaca products made here in New England. The product is made from pure alpaca fiber which was grown on our farm from our herd of alpacas. Each year they are sheared in the spring before it gets too warm out. The fiber is then processed into products. Alpaca fiber is softer than cashmere and warmer than wool. The fiber is also hypo-allergenic and antibacterial.

Alpacas have been in South America in the Andes Mountains Plains for over 5,000 years. The Incas treasured the fiber for the royalty as it was considered the best natural fabric in the world. Today, Alpaca clothing is passed down from generation to generation. Alpaca fiber is a green and organic product. Welcome to The Green Revolution.

Winter Scene

Here in New England, the winters can be harsh and very cold. Winter here on the farm can be a struggle to survive. We now have a multitude of renewable energy systems in operation to help with the cold, hard months.

On the farm it is very peaceful in the real rural part of America. This is what they call serenity. The price of having this is long hours of hard work, along with lots of effort and planning. This property was raw forested land when my wife and I first got it. From there. we built the farm for alpacas. The alpacas help to enhance this wholesome scene.

Polish Fancy Chickens and Roosters

Here are great pets for a farm. They roam free about our farm, clean up anyspilled grain, and eat bugs and ticks. The alpacas love their presence, too. The chickens and roosters also enjoy the presence of other birds. In the early morning, the rooster is our alarm clock at the farm. Each evening, the Polish fancies move into their coop to stay away from predators and to lay eggs for us to eat. Save energy and buy a rooster instead of an alarm clock.

The Arabian Horse

The Arabian horse is known for its loyalty, strength, good disposition, and unwavering endurance. These horses are well-known throughout the world as excellent long-distance runners. They can trek 50-100 miles a day in just about any geographic region or climate on Earth. The Arabian horse that we adopted is named Omir, or Omi for short. Most of our animals are rescued from previous owners that have passed on or lost interest in these fine animals. At our farm, the animals use our implemented renewable energy resources for their survival and, in turn, give us unwavering love, companionship, respect, and friendship. Omi uses our solar electric fence to keep out any unwanted predators and helps contribute manure for fertilizer and methane production.

350.org

350.org is an international organization of individuals who agree that the world must have a maximum atmospheric carbon dioxide (CO_2) level of 350 parts per million (ppm) in order to stop the climate from warming more than it already has. Today, scientists say that the atmospheric CO_2 level is at 390 ppm. Our polar region's temperatures are increasing the fastest because there is less white snow and ice covering them. White surfaces reflect heat, while black or darker colors absorb heat. Some of our regions at the poles are now raw, dark landmasses. The ice caps, glaciers, and polar regions are warming at an alarming rate. Chunks of ice shelves the size of Rhode Island are breaking off in Antarctica. Greenland is also melting into the North Atlantic Sea and releasing methane hydrates into the atmosphere. This causes more than 20 times the release of CO_2 than burning fossil fuels.

Over 150 countries have more than 5,000 renewable and sustainable projects going on concurrently. They are doing this to prove to their nations and to the rest of the world that using natural and renewable resources comes with responsibility.

Let this be a lesson to all governments, individuals, and humanity that we need to change the way we use our resources here on the planet and establish more renewable and sustainable ways.

Zen Tower

I found these rocks when we dug the hole for the solar array pole foundations. I had studied Zen philosophy during my martial arts career in Taekwondo and during my enlightenment and heightened awareness exercises, I made this Zen tower in the front yard.

References

www.projectfeeds.info

Massachusetts Institute of Technology, MIT

University of Connecticut Global Fuel Cell Center

University Of Hartford

University Of Wisconsin

Manchester Community College

www.HelioCentris.com

www.rissyplastics.com

www.Cthydro.com

www.Waldorenewable.com

www.Nutmegmechanical.com

www.Backwoodsolar.com

www.Ctcleanenergy.org

www.paulnashphotography.com

www.Reneact.org

www.Pace-cleanenergy.org

www.ClimatePartners.com

www.Webcontentrx.com

Charles Fowler: maidintheshade@hotmail.com

www.CarbonFootprint.com

www.Cleantechnica.com

Climate-2030-report

www.350.org

www.greenoptimistic.com

www.ctsolarlease.org

www.youtube.com (Project FEEDS and The Mr. Norm Show)

www.windspire.com

www.solarhydrogensystems.com

www.apricussolar.com

Green, Greener, Greenest by Lori Bongiorno

www.erenewable.biz

www.ecover.com/us/en/

180 Things That Project FEEDS and Norman Nadeau Do to Save Energy, Generate Green Power, and Educate the Public

> *"This is how we are going to combat global warming. Here are 180 ways to lower your carbon footprint and help humanity's survival now and for generations to come."*
>
> — Mr. Norman A. Nadeau
> Visionary, Philosopher, Green Advocate, Revolutionary

1. Project FEEDS (Friendly Environmental Energy Dependent Systems) and I appeared on the front page of local and national newspapers regarding going green and being sustainable by treading softly on our environment. See www.projectfeeds.info.

2. I wrote up Project FEEDS to plan for fossil-fuel-free electric energy production.

3. Our home, farm, and Project FEEDS have a negative carbon footprint and are educating others on how to become carbon-neutral or carbon-negative. The average person puts 1. 4 tons (2,800 pounds) of CO_2 into the atmosphere each year.

4. Project FEEDS is educational as I give sustainable energy tours to anyone who wishes to learn about renewable energy at a functioning demonstration facility.

5. I created a website to increase awareness about renewable energy.

6. We added sustainable renewable energy links to our website. We added education, services, and renewable energy products. See www. erenewable.biz.

7. We support proposed legislation for tax credits on cars and trucks converted to hybrids and received practical response back from a Senator.

8. We joined 350.org and offer tours and education on the green movement. (Note: 350.org is dedicated to reducing 350 parts per million of CO_2 emissions in the atmosphere.)

9. We installed an 8kw (8,000 watt) grid-tied solar voltaic array. We used grant funding with leasing which led to a reduction in energy costs.

10. We use solar-powered LED lights on the farm. Just about everywhere, they can be seen lighting up the ranch and farm.

11. We use solar LED lights in our home.

12. We've changed the light bulbs in our home to compact fluorescent (or LED) lights. If everybody in America changed just one light bulb in their home to compact fluorescent or LED, it would be equivalent to taking one million cars off the road.

13. We installed LED's on our farm tractor as a more efficient source of light for evening farm jobs.

14. We use a solar-powered charger to recharge our batteries. The solar charger was once a solar light that someone discarded. I recycled it and now use it to charge rechargeable batteries.

15. I wear a solar-powered watch to eliminate waste from batteries in our dumps. I am now wearing the next generation solar watch, which costs ten times less than the first solar watches years ago.

16. Our home contains windows of increased size to allow more solar heating of our home (especially on the south side facing for maximum sunlight).

17. We sealed our home to reduce heat loss in winter and heat intrusion in summer, which reduced heating and cooling costs. The cost and work was

done by a local state-funded eco-solutions program called Connecticut Clean Energy Options and Connecticut Clean Energy Fund. These programs exist in just about every state in the United States.

18. We use a heat-powered Ecofan™ on our wood stove to circulate warm air and reduce the amount of wood needed to heat our home. The fan operates via a thermocouple which provides electricity from heat.

19. We use an energy-efficient Energy Star cook-top stove. These ovens can be found at most stores.

20. We use an energy-efficient Energy Star microwave. These ovens can be found at most appliance stores.

21. We purchased an energy-efficient Energy Star refrigerator. We keep it more than half-full to reduce its energy consumption.

22. We produce hydrogen on-site for our electric generating fuel. We use PEM (proton exchange membrane) fuel cells to charge our small batteries.

23. We recycle all containers and/or reuse them. Most plastic containers (used only when completely necessary) can be reused or recycled.

24. We use reusable plastic sandwich containers. Always wash the container before reusing them.

25. We clean and reuse plastic cutlery at parties. Some can be recycled or re-used if sanitized properly.

26. We clean and reuse plastic drinking cups.

27. We use paper instead of plastic whenever possible.

28. We use stainless steel water bottles to limit use of plastic bottles.

29. Sometimes we drink soda and other drinks from recycled plastics.

30. We substantially reduced our dependency on plastic products.

31. We now get a deposit on all water bottles here in Connecticut and most states in New England. This green revolution of recycling is spreading all over the United States and other nations as well. Finally, there will be less water bottles on the side of the road. I write with a pen that is made

from two water bottles and writes in black soy ink. So, there you have it, recycle your water bottles if you use them.

32. We use stainless steel travel mugs. They can be reused many times and are very durable.

33. We use coffee mugs, not throw away cups. Try to avoid Styrofoam cups.

34. We use eco-friendly reusable bags when grocery shopping. Most people are using these bags today to reduce plastic and paper bag waste.

35. We reuse our feed grain bags from our farm for garbage bags and also use them to transport seasoned manure for gardening. Seasoned manure is a great replacement for fertilizer, which may harm the environment.

36. We hang our wet clothes outside on a clothesline to save the energy needed to dry them. This reduces the need for electricity to dry clothes.

37. We hang clothes on racks inside during bad weather instead of using a dryer.

38. We unplug appliances when not in use to prevent wasted electricity. There are a lot of appliances that have ghost electricity when not in use. If possible, use an electric power strip to shut off electronics that use power when not in use.

39. We use reusable air filters in our automobiles. These filters can be purchased at most auto parts stores. They will let your engine breathe better, thus giving your car more power and mileage per gallon.

40. We installed a solar thermal greenhouse to provide year-round vegetables. Growing your own food when possible allows you to be less dependent on outside sources for fresh food and vegetables.

41. We created a hydroponic gardening system to grow vegetables and fruits.

42. We grow our own organic vegetables. Knowing that your food came from your own hands is a good feeling.

43. We grow some of our own organic fruits in a solar greenhouse and around our property. Growing your own fruit helps not only your family's need for food, but also eliminates the need for diesel trucks to transport fruit

to your local stores. This saves usage of fossil fuels, which results in less pollution of our environment.

44.   We buy organic food whenever possible.

45.   We use organic eggs from local farms and reuse the egg cartons. We also have our own chickens for our own personal egg production.

46.   We had taken one fruit and vegetable from each of our crops and saved the seeds to be replanted for the following year. This is a sustainable way of growing food crops.

47.   We plant trees and bushes that produce fruit. We are creating an edible landscape where everything that grows can be eaten.

48.   We have made maple syrup at our ranch by collecting the sap during the season, then storing, filtering, and boiling it down to pure and natural maple syrup. This year, we made enough to last us over a year. Pancakes, anyone?

49.   We occasionally grill our food outside using clean, natural gas or home-grown methane instead of using electric heat or microwave ovens. We also cook outside with our camp synthesis gas stove which emits near-zero emissions.

50.   We try to buy green products from environmentally-friendly companies.

51.   We have a rain water collector for home and farm use. This is for emergency drinking and is used as distilling water for my fuel cells. It is easy to set up rain water collectors and some systems use underground tanks.

52.   We only use air conditioning when absolutely necessary. Instead of using air conditioning, we open our windows to get fresh air.

53.   We don't leave our air conditioner on when we are not at home. Leaving an air conditioner on when no humans are present is a waste of energy. Installing a timer on your air conditioner is practical because it ensures that the unit will only be running when people are home.

54.   We limit the time we spend in the shower to save water. Each of us uses

a timer to limit hot water usage. Once the timer goes off, we know it's time to finish our shower. Remember, our hot water is supported by a solar thermal system which provides 90% of our hot water.

55. Our farm uses old hoses that would have been thrown away to reduce solid waste. We repair the leaks and re-use them for gardening purposes and for transporting water to the farm animals for drinking water. We also use old hoses to repair our current hose system. I know of a friend that re-uses black hose by layering it in a field to transport hot water back to his home.

56. Our farm uses a solar electric fence. This fence uses solar electricity rather than ordinary electricity, thus saving lots of energy. This is also renewable each day over and over, year after year.

57. On our farm, we use a fuel-efficient diesel tractor that was converted into a hydrogen hybrid diesel. Just be sure to get a tractor that is suited to the needs of your farm or ranch facility. That way, you will not over-do the size of the machine for the job and you will use less diesel and oil.

58. We use synthetic oil in our diesel farm tractor. This further protects the engine from wear, which will make it last longer than usual.

59. We reuse hay bailing string as temporary halters for our horses and alpacas. We also use it as a stringer for fishing, to tie up a tent, or to tie up fencing on the farm. There are many uses for hay bailing string, yet most farmers simply throw it away.

60. We compost the farm's animal manure for fertilizer. We no longer have to buy fertilizer that may harm the water supply down the road or in the river.

61. We do not use pesticides or fertilizer on the farm or on our home.

62. We reuse boxes to store items on the farm and in our home. Cardboard has many uses and can also now be recycled.

63. Our telephones can be recharged more than one thousand times. Thanks to technology and easy recharging, a phone can be recharged just about anywhere today.

64. Old clothes, if unsuitable for donation, are reused as rags.

65. Clothes that are in good condition are donated to charity.

66. We shop for clothes at thrift stores and consignment shops before we purchase new items.

67. We use rechargeable, wireless computer mice for our computers.

68. We donated a small solar panel to a homeless man so that he could recharge batteries.

69. We use the fiber harvested from our alpacas to make clothes. Alpacas re-grow their fiber every year, which can be harvested without harming the animal.

70. Alpacas are our lawnmowers on the farm. They eat the grass down to about an inch so that we never have to use a gas-guzzling lawnmower.

71. I bought reused oil that was recycled by collection from oil change and repair facilities. Some people who cannot afford to purchase synthetic oil can now buy recycled oil which is also very clean to use. It is recycled and remade here in the United States. I still recommend full synthetic oil for better efficiency and protection for your engines.

72. We finally retired our gas lawnmower, our hydrogen hybrid mower and replaced it with an efficient electric lawnmower. This mower works great and completes the job for what lawn I have left in our front yard.

73. We use the wood chips from logging as mulch on our property. We also use the wood chips to make synthesis gas for cooking.

74. We use washable and re-usable coffee cups at home, on the farm, and at the office.

75. We purchase recycled and/or used books and then recycle them when they are no longer needed or donate them to charity. Some new books are being made of recycled materials, and the digital age has helped reduce paper use as well.

76. We shut off lights in rooms that are not being used. Timers and sensors can now be used to help your family save energy.

77. We purchase electricity from a green provider. When your electric bill comes in each month, you have a choice of using green energy.

78. We use natural organic shampoo to bathe our dogs and cats.

79. We use flashlights that are rechargeable.

80. Our flashlights use LED technology for long life, energy efficiency, and bright light.

81. Each year, we purchase an organically-raised steer for our family. This steer provides us with chemically-free lean meat.

82. Each year, we raise an organic pig for family consumption, which we then also share with another local family. We have also pooled our local resources by sharing our organically grown food. In doing so, we've helped other people to choose to eat and grow local food organically.

83. We properly disposed of an old, inefficient freezer and purchased an energy-efficient freezer.

84. We integrated our renewable energy systems to reduce the intermittent use of renewable energy systems like solar, wind, and hydrogen with any combination of these systems. We have also applied for provisional patent rights for this system.

85. We had a local contractor install indirect solar thermal heating and a hot water system to provide 90% (or more) of our heat and hot water needs.

86. We recycle ink cartridges from our copiers. A redemption fee is now paid to recycle ink cartridges.

87. We wear sweaters in the winter to save heating costs and save energy. Throw on an extra blanket or a sweater in the colder months of the year to help you save energy.

88. We try to eliminate most, if not all, paper catalogs and use online catalogs instead.

89. We shop online for many items and consumables to save on traveling to stores.

90. We converted our diesel car to a hydrogen hybrid. This reduced emissions to almost zero, eliminated black exhaust, and almost doubled the life of the engine, it's incredible.

91. We no longer use petroleum-based motor oil for our cars. We now use synthetic oil that is made in America and change it every 10,000 miles. This helps us reduce oil consumption substantially.

92. We are using on-board automotive fuel cell technology to generate hydrogen from water and vinegar: the benefits include better mileage, increased horsepower, and a reduction of emissions to almost zero.

93. We converted our gas cars to hydrogen hybrid technology to save fuel, have clean emissions, more power, and make the engine last much longer.

94. We retired our sport utility vehicle (SUV). It went to auction for some else to reuse and we have now replaced it with a hydrogen diesel pickup.

95. We drive our vehicles only when we must.

96. We simply walk instead of using a car when possible.

97. We sometimes commute together to reduce CO_2.

98. I work at home one day per week instead of commuting.

99. We eat less fried food.

100. We support green organizations.

101. We created a blog about the reality of global warming and how to combat it on a micro-scale.

102. We reuse old solar panels for small energy projects around the home and farm.

103. We create and use methane from a compost pile to prevent it from being released into the atmosphere.

104. We use less paper newspapers by reading them online instead.

105. We recycle as much of our household and farm waste as possible. It is at least 50% less than last year, which means we are recycling more of our

waste from farm and residence.

106. We use extra blankets on our beds during the winter to reduce the need to use the heat overnight.

107. We catch our own bait for fishing.

108. We sometimes pick up after others who are not ecologically conscious so that plastics, aluminum cans, and glass bottles are properly disposed of.

109. I contain petroleum from being released into the ocean when boating.

110. We recycle our office environment waste paper, plastics, and cardboard.

111. We grow new grass each year to be used as feed on our farm.

112. We drive our vehicles at or below posted speed limits to save fuel when we can.

113. We use all-natural sponges for washing our boat and vehicles.

114. We utilize our cold basement air to cool our home in the summer.

115. We use disposable, recyclable writing pens.

116. We gave disposable pens to close friends to show how things can be recycled.

117. Whenever possible, we reuse stationary and envelopes for our home use and copier rather than only using it once. Sometimes recycling must come from creative thinking.

118. We use common household natural cleaning solvents which are environmentally-friendly, such as white vinegar. Vinegar, when used properly, can be a great glass cleaner.

119. We inherited a wind turbine electric generator and installed it to provide power for our farm and home.

120. We buy gasoline from oil companies that promote renewable energy.

121. We recycled and reused European pine four-by-four beams which came from Germany via an airbus cargo transport plane. The beams were left

at the airport after deliveries from overseas to reduce the weight of the airbus plane, thus saving fuel, when returning to Europe. I was offered the beams just before they were to be thrown away. We constructed a very sturdy barn at our ranch facility using those beams. It goes to show now that things made by man can be used over and over with good creativity of thought.

122. We use recycled paper on the farm, in our residence, and in my professional activities at the office.

123. A great way to save on paper at the office is to offer electronic delivery of documents. For example, I offer my customers a choice between electronic delivery service or paper and normal mail delivery when sending business documents.

124. We buy gift cards printed on recycled paper.

125. We reuse large envelopes.

126. We shred all used paper in the office and recycle it.

127. My financial and insurance office is now using less than 50% of the paper that it did two years ago. We now recycle all paper and plastic at the office.

128. We went 50% paperless at home.

129. We use recycled shoelaces.

130. We wash our cars by hand instead of going to the car wash to save energy.

131. We separate waste paper to be recycled instead of throwing it away at the office.

132. Some of our mail comes in recycled paper envelopes.

133. We have reduced our need to print documents at the office substantially, which saves paper and helps us migrate to a paperless office.

134. We buy soft drinks in bulk to cut down on plastic containers.

135. We choose paper instead of Styrofoam for soft drinks.

136. We use environmentally-friendly soap.

137. We use environmentally-friendly soap to wash our boat and cars.

138. I joined the environmental global movement towards climate change.

139. We purchase organic cotton shirts and clothing.

140. We use environmentally-friendly bottom paint for our boat.

141. We use environmentally-friendly antifreeze for our automobiles.

142. We drink organically-grown coffee and tea.

143. We use batteries from vehicles donated by a local construction company for our renewable energy project's back-up power.

144. We use teleconferencing to save energy and time at the office.

145. We recycled our plastic mailbox when it needed replacement.

146. We primarily drink soda or other drinks in recyclable aluminum.

147. I use an oxygen fuel cell for aeration of a fish tank. This is a new way to provide oxygen to fish, which uses substantially less energy.

148. We obtain and reuse plastic pipe around our farm and home.

149. We do not use Teflon cookware because it is toxic.

150. I set up south side magnetism on hydrocarbon fuel lines to realign molecules to burn fuel more efficiently. These super strong earth magnets provide hydrogen molecules from a negative valence to a positive valence. See this on our YouTube video at www.youtube.com/user/projectFEEDS#p/u/19/TV9JTfmTVQ.

151. We set up south side magnets to soften the water at our home.

152. I've inspired people to learn and adapt to renewable and sustainable living needs.

153. I inspired and educated an elementary school on how to be more efficient with energy and, most of all, I had the students participate in recycling

plastics, paper, and cardboard to be environmentally friendly.

154. We use small inverters in our car and truck to recharge our computers and gadgets that need more power and are renewable. Sometimes you need energy suddenly while you are traveling. It is a wise choice to carry a small inverter made for trucks and cars to create the energy you need to recharge any device that has depleted its own energy source.

155. Plant a tree. Planting trees helps the environment and gives us more oxygen to breathe. Trees store our carbon dioxide in wood, they act as carbon collectors of pollution, and also release oxygen into our atmosphere.

156. Americans use 70 million gallons of liquid hydrogen for automotive fuel every year; we are proposing that people produce hydrogen on-site for many applications. We have also decided to educate people on how to safely make hydrogen onboard a vehicle.

157. We recycle furniture that only needs small repairs. We have nice leather chairs that people had abandoned because they were in need of a small repair. Normally, these chairs would cost hundreds of dollars in a store. Recovering something and knowing you can fix it warrants a good recycling habit of re-using things.

158. We use organic sugar for our coffee and tea.

159. Our family and business works with ecologically-conscious energy providers whenever we can.

160. We are an ecologically-friendly electrical energy generator.

161. Our energy project is a member of our town's Green Team Task Force, helping the community save energy and become more environmentally conscious by lowering its dependence on fossil fuels.

162. Project FEEDS joined a sustainable renewable energy commission in my town to help create change in our local community and government on sustainable energy projects.

163. Leading by example, our neighbor installed a solar, grid-tied electric generation system. When a home goes green, it shows others a path so they can do it too.

164. I convinced my neighbor to install an efficient tank-less water heater to save on CO_2 emissions. Heating hot water is now feasible through many means of renewable energy.

165. My son, Alex, and I made YouTube videos to educate people about renewable energy. They are "The Mr. Norm Show" and "Projectfeeds". See www.youtube.com/user/ProjectFEEDS.

166. I teach renewable energy and sustainability to adults and children in my community. If you teach children, they will go home and teach their parents solutions for a greener world.

167. I show people how to add hydrogen hybrid technology to their vehicles. This saves energy, increases mileage, increases power, and makes their vehicles more environmentally friendly.

168. I showed local truck and car repair shops how to install and service hydrogen hybrids, and hybrids in general, thus creating a new service industry.

169. I spurred economic development for renewable energy and sustainability by promoting the hiring of unemployed people to work toward a greener environment.

170. I inspired engineers and Ph.D.'s to be more proactive in our green revolution, in renewable energy, and in sustainable technologies.

171. I give lectures on sustainability and renewable energy.

172. I reach out to my financial clients to go green and save CO_2 from being released into the air.

173. I gave high-tech lectures at an adult education conference so that individuals can become re-educated for green, sustainable jobs for their future.

174. I consult with multinational corporations in Pakistan and India on how to bring energy to villages, towns, and cities via renewable systems.

175. We use deodorant which does not have aluminum in it.

176. We use Eco-friendly aluminum foil packaging.

177. We properly dispose of light bulbs that contain mercury.

178. We use eco-friendly dishwater detergent, made by Full Circle™.

179. I created a remote-controlled device to control the operation of our farm's energy supply from a single location.

180. Our farm is totally powered by renewable energy. Try to grow your own food and make your own energy. How carbon neutral are you?

Credits

Most photographs by Paul Nash Photography,
www.Paulnashphotography.com

Additional photos by Norman A. Nadeau

Photo of solar eclipse of moon: Image per GNU free documentation license version 1.2 and per creative commons attribution share alike 3.0 Author Oliver Stein

Cover by Melanie Garmon, Printwise, LLC; www.printwiseLLC.com; Melanie@printwiseLLC.com

Solar Insolation Chart

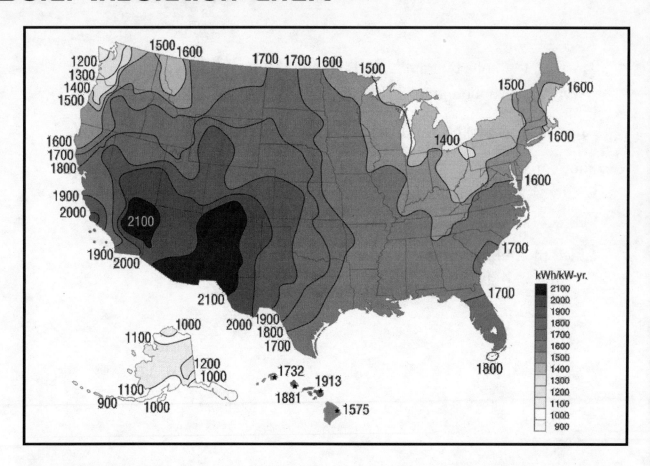

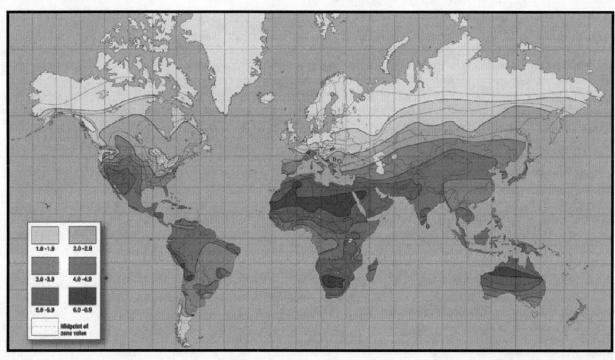